MY MISSION STATEMENT

'To connect women to the moon cycles and the
seasons. Releasing stress and overwhelm, to restore
balance, motivation, gain clarity, direction, and align
to your goddess power. Readying you to sparkle and
shine, dancing through your life and spreading your
unique medicine and magic.'

Moon 2023 Goddess diary

NORTHERN HEMISPHERE

THIS DIARY BELONGS TO THIS GORGEOUS BEING:

_____

ROCKPOOL

Darling one,

Loving you is a sacred and special gift I share with you, just you.

Loving you fills me with such strength, for in you I see my potential to be brighter, sparklier and more gorgeous each day.

Loving you reminds me that I am not alone in this world. I am deeply connected to someone so magnificent, gorgeous, loving and kind.

Loving you inspires me to stretch, to grow, to be radiantly sexy, to find pleasure in how I shine and to own my goddess nature.

Loving you means that, perhaps in the moments of your greatest need, where you forget your powers and amazingness, I show up to love you and hold you while you remember who you truly are.

Loving you was something that I was always destined to do. We made a pact.

Loving you means that the soft place of your dreams is where I feel the most connected to you.

Loving you means that, even when you turn away from yourself and from me, I keep showing up, waiting for you to find me once more. For all these moments, I love you still. I always will, my darling.

Grandmother Moon xx

PS: Should you ever feel the need for that extra support or big beaming sign of love or reminder that you are incredibly important and so worthy of being seen, you only need to look up. I'm always here.

ABOUT THE AUTHOR

Hey!

I'm Nicci, a moon dancer, ocean soul, goddess, mother, lover, pleasure seeker and creator of fun, who is dedicated to helping you become the woman you most want to be.

I am a transformational speaker, kinesiologist, medical intuitive and energy healer, who is incredibly connected to the angelic realm and to the beautiful mother earth wisdom, to all those shamanic guides and practices.

My husband and four children (Summer-Rose, Harmony, Trinity and Maverick) are the focus of my world, and not a day goes by that I am not wowed by the love and support they all give to me.

I'm an Aussie girl who tries to breathe fun and pleasure into my day. I love to feel beautiful, sexy, fulfilled and supported. I have a dream that ALL women should allow themselves to rise up. To embrace their divine feminine and connection to their soul, their goddess energy and living from this profoundly magical space.

I'm proud to have created this diary that inspires women all over the world to feel connected to the cycles of the moon and the seasons. To feel worthy and ready to live from their highest potential by 'tuning in' to their desires and prioritizing themselves.

Women are often raised and encouraged to fit into this world by being the caregivers, the nurturers, playing small, being a certain size, or shelving their dreams for the sake of their family. So often, we shelve our natural way of doing things, the way of feeling into something, our intuition and our fun for the benefit of others.

For me, here is where I found the moon; she guided me back to myself when I had become lost on my journey of trying to answer the question 'Who am I?'. This was an awakening for me.

This diary encourages you to be you, all of who you are. We will help you find the way back inside. I've done it and you can too!

I am so honored to have you join me for this year. It's going to be powerful, magical and completely awesome.

Nicci xx

INTRODUCTION

I started these diaries because full moons are the perfect opportunity and gift to each of us to release, let go and clear away anything that you feel is no longer in *your* highest good. I used to go down to my local beach and sit under the Full Moon two to three times a year to balance my body, my cycles, my emotions, my systems. I'd meditate, walk in the sand, stand with the waves licking over my feet – a bit like hitting a reset button, just for me.

It was a wonderful reason to have a whole hour to myself without the kids, too! My clients were looking for similar things to help them hit their reset buttons so they could discover their sacred space or ceremony to come back to themselves.

In December 2016, I started my Full Moon Meditations, offering my clients the opportunity to come down to the local beach where I lived in Queensland, Australia, to meditate under a Full Moon. That first month we had 20 people come. We watched the moon rise and, as I held the space for these women, we meditated together. Within three months, we had over 100 people coming. Just outside of a year, we reached over 2,500 people filling the beach. In January 2019, we had over 4,500 people attend that night.

The moon really does affect us all. By choosing to harness this energy, by having the awareness found throughout the course of this diary and by accessing your Goddess self-care toolkit, you will feel balanced, aligned and supported. You will thrive and become the empowered woman you are destined to be.

I see you,

Nicci xx

> PS: The 2023 edition of this dairy was written in a little shack called 'Studio 54', in a little town called Brunswick Heads near Byron Bay. It is infused with extra healing powers extracted from all around the northern rivers in NSW, Australia, as well as the oceans, mountains, beaches, people and plant medicine of this beautiful place.

HOW TO USE THIS DIARY

This diary is written with the intention that you write, draw, color, paint, paste and doodle in it. Its pages are longing for you to fill them each week with sprinkles of your love. Sometimes when you get a new diary, this little part inside of you stirs up. It's a resistance to actually putting anything in your pages that may not be right or good enough, that may be judged, be imperfect, or that you feel ashamed about, regret putting in, etc etc. It's all just your fears (usually from when you were at school) about being imperfect and not enough.

Let's do a quick ritual to bring healing to this area, so that you are free to play, express and communicate throughout the course of your diary, but also your year.

Hold your diary open (it doesn't matter at which page) and start to breathe deeply, in and out. Settle into your body with your calming breath, slow it down and allow your breath to find a rhythm of its own.

Surround yourself, your diary and the whole space around you with a beautiful purple light. This purple light completely surrounds you with an upgraded, safer and more potent way for you to express yourself through your diary. It activates your capacity to connect to those inner parts of your heart and intuitive self, so you can be more open to expressing yourself in ways that you love. This purple light is the color of spirituality and it will stay with you throughout your journey of 2023.

Scrawling, scribbling, gluing, messy, neat, organized, print, SHOUTING CAPITALS, curse words, drawing, stick figures, pictures, images, color, textas, crayons, kid's drawings, stickers, post-it notes, cut-outs, words, quotes, incorrect grammar, punctuation and spelling mistakes are all welcomed and allowed to be present within the pages of your diary. And it is so.

Call in the magic and medicine of the 12 sacred goddesses who have been channeled to support you this year with their guidance, their love and their radiance; call in Oshun, Kuan Yin, Arianrhod, Isis, Mama Quilla, Archangel Haniel, Ix Chel, Luna, Selene, Anahita, Freya and Hina Hine – and weave in their magic even more throughout your whole body and the pages of your diary.

Take three deep breaths to come back into this moment, feeling excited to play in your diary and supported by your 12 goddesses throughout 2023. Gosh, it's going to be such an exciting year for you.

Nicci xx

MY GODDESS SELF-CARE TOOLKIT FOR WINTER

All moon goddesses and professionals have tools that help them do their job better, easier, quicker or smarter, like secret weapons of support. Creating a few really specific, powerful and different self-care tools will help bring you the support you need to cope and thrive through each season of this year. These tools will help you show up to be the best version of yourself each day.

Life gets messy, drama happens, things don't always go as planned, you get emotional, the moon stirs the energy up and some days you can feel like 'it's all too much'. Having the tools to support you through these times is what propels you through them, rather than falling in a heap of 'why bother' or 'I can't do this anymore'. These tools help you stay in the moment of your life and reconnect to your inner potency of awesomeness. They will help you find your magic and sparkle.

You outgrow things that support you because you are always changing and growing and shifting. You will find yourself choosing different tools to support you for each season. You will notice your personal shift and also notice how your needs change with each season. And that's important.

With tingles of excitement deep in your belly, let's get started!

Winter is the time of retreat, clearing and taking the time to get to know yourself deeper so you may be reborn in the spring, stronger and ready to sparkle.

All the self-care tools you choose here will support you from today until the Spring Equinox in March. These self-care tools will help you thrive throughout your winter season with extra sprinkles of love and magic.

There are no right or wrong answers. Let go of your answers being any better, for they are all just your perfectly imperfect answers for today. Take five big breaths, really filling up your lungs, then let all your breath out. Imagine a slippery dip is going from your thinking mind into your heart space. Feel yourself sliding down and landing in your heart. Open your heart space a little wider (even if you are unsure if you're doing it right, trust that you are) — that's it!

GODDESS

Let's start with choosing a goddess. Flip through until you come to January, February and March. Really notice the picture of each goddess and read the description about her. Which goddess feels like she will help you the most this season?

_____

The goddess I have chosen to support me throughout winter 2023 is

_____

She will support me with the medicine of her

_____

COLOR

Choose one color that is going to support you throughout winter. Land on your color and write it down here:

_____

When I see this color, I feel

_____

I can use this color to support me throughout winter with things such as clothing, accessories, jewelry, flowers, scatter cushions, candles, crystals, pens and

_____

SONGS

Choose three upbeat songs. Songs that you love, songs that get you up and moving, songs that make you feel that it's impossible to stay completely still, songs that make you feel like you want to boom-shakka-lakka and shimmy-shake around your house.

When you feel irritated, what could you do to get those deep irritations and emotions out of your body? You can dance them out! Yes, I know it sounds a little bit weird (okay, super weird) but it really does work.

If I am feeling a little triggered, angry, scared, irritated or just in a funk, I can play these three songs so I can get all loose and not caring, and allow the music and dance to move me through the emotion.

My three songs are:

1. _____

2. _____

3. _____

Your song mission is to download your three songs and create a special winter playlist on your phone so that, whenever you need them, they are ready for you.

EXERCISE

Don't moan when you read the word 'exercise'. It will be okay, I promise. Moving your body is important: you know that, I know that, everyone knows that. If there was a magical place that you could visit and it would transform your body with the push of a button, we'd all go there, right? Unfortunately, I am yet to discover this place so, for now, we all have to move our bodies to keep them strong and bendy in the ways we have available to us at this moment.

Make this exercise as joyful, pleasurable, enlightening and as fun as it can be. There are so many ways to move your body. Choose one that feels exciting for you now.

The ways I will move my body during winter are:

_____

I will do these at _____ (location), _____ times per week.

FRAGRANCE

Your nose is a powerful tool. When you smell something you love, your whole body can feel so happy. It is like your nose holds this secret power to connect you to what brings you pleasure. You even have memories triggered by your sense of smell. In choosing to notice these scents you love, and by sprinkling them throughout your day, you will trigger a pleasure response that reminds you to feel all loved up and amazing. Kinda cool, hey!

For winter, choose one smell that is going to support you throughout this season. It could be an essential oil, a perfume, a flower. Choose something you just love, that is easy to use and fills you with pleasure.

Land on your fragrance and write it down here:

_____

When your nostrils are tickled with this fragrance, how do you feel?

_____

I can use this fragrance as my signature winter scent to support me in lots of ways such as burning essential oils and candles, using in skincare, eating or cooking with it, wearing the perfume, smelling fresh flowers, as well as

_____ and _____

CRYSTALS

Crystals are like magical particles that hold healing powers within. There are thousands of crystals available and they all have individual characteristics or ways to support you. Using the magic of one crystal helps to guide you with what you are working on, with healing, clearing or reminding you how you are growing and what you are wanting to step into.

The crystal I am choosing to support me for winter is called

_____

It is _____ (color) and it will help me to _____

I can use this crystal to support me in lots of ways, such as carrying a piece in my pocket, or keeping a piece in the car or my bag. I could wear it in jewelry, use it as a screensaver on my phone, pop it under my pillow or mattress to support me while I sleep, or I could

_____ or _____

MANTRA

By now, you know what you are working on and how you would like to feel. Have a look at the goddesses from January, February and March. Choose one of the mantras they have sent to you.

I am learning how to

_____

Your special mantra mission is to write your affirmation on post-it notes and sprinkle these words around your home, work office, phone and car. Write it down every week in this diary until the Spring Equinox to remind you to say it. Write it in lipstick on your mirror or in your journal, or perhaps you could

_____

For an extra gold star for being amazing, fill in three things you love most about winter.

1._____

2._____

3._____

I will choose to do these things more because they bring me pleasure and fill my heart with joy. I deserve joy. (Yes, you really do!)

Well done. That is your very own Goddess self-care toolkit for winter all finished and completed. It will be here to support you through to the Spring Equinox in March.

Call in your goddess and play your three boppy songs now, swaying those hips as you dance and twirl around in celebration of completing your toolkit.

JANUARY

OSHUN

Your Moon Goddess for January is the gorgeous Oshun.

Oshun (Osun) is a West African Moon Goddess of love, beauty, sensuality, divinity and fertility – she embodies love, not any type of love we are used to, but a rare undying, unconditional 'I love you with every fiber of my being' type of love. She has great warrior strength inside her, incredible mystical and healing capabilities, and she loves to dance to the rhythm of the music of the world.

She is divinely beautiful, with a naturally gorgeous and bold afro hairstyle and flawless skin of deep brown. She has a luscious, full, sexy, womanly figure that oozes sensuality and charisma. Notice the way Oshun holds her head, notice her eyes, notice how she owns every part of who she is and almost challenges you to do the same – this invitation to be divine.

Oshun can feel into the depths of your soul and see where you are not living your divine purpose. She can see your gifts and talents, and where you are not using these sacred gifts. She can also see your warrior strength, your radiant beauty, the light that resides within you – your divinity, your potency.

She has come through this month to support you to reach a new level of self-acceptance and to help you participate in this ancient ritual of transformation with her. She is calling you to your 'more'.

Oshun's mantra is 'I am learning how to accept myself just as I am, in this breath, this moment, this day, this moon cycle.'

Her crystals are honey calcite, labradorite and fancy jasper.

Her totems are peacock feathers – to be boldly you, and mirrors – to see your radiant beauty reflected back at you.

Her exercise is dancing – to move your body to the beat of your drum.

Her scent is honey – for the sweetness of life.

27 TUESDAY

28 WEDNESDAY

As the end of the year looms near, it's rather easy to launch into your list of resolutions for 2023.
   Could you give yourself permission to hold off on this for a little while? You are still becoming aligned to the shifts of the Winter Solstice and the New Moon and you are still receiving the healing and the clearing. It is important to close this year 2022 off first.

29 THURSDAY

30 FRIDAY

31 SATURDAY

Place your hands on your heart and start to breathe deeply. Love the person you are today. Appreciate your journey through the 365 days of the year that you have lived through. Give thanks to those in your life who supported you this year. Give thanks to the cycles of the moon for supporting you through this whole year and holding your hand, to guide you.

1 SUNDAY   JANUARY 2023

Happy New Year, beautiful one. Twirl around with your arms open wide and fully stretched out to the possibility of this year. 2023 is going to be amazing and powerful, your best and most fabulous year yet. Feel into that excitement, that possibility and that hope.

2 MONDAY

3 TUESDAY

In numerology, 2023 is a number 7: 2+0+2+3=7. The themes for number 7 years are spirituality, intuition, introspection, faith and inner peace. Your focus in 2022 was 'where do I belong', what 'home' means to you, and connecting to a sense of harmony in your world. In 2023, there'll be the opportunity for you to begin moving forward in your life with a stronger connection and deeper meaning to what you want.

   You have this beautiful energy of looking within for the answers you seek, but also a support team for you to start using more throughout your life. It's the year to start noticing more and trusting more in the journey of your life. Seeing how the universe sends you support – through nature, in sunsets, a feather, crystals, rocks, songs, words, books, people, diaries and so many other ways – that you are deeply loved.

4 WEDNESDAY

5 THURSDAY

Oshun's message for you – 'Today I stand here fully in my body, open to receiving transformation and insights.' Twirl that in through your body.

6 FRIDAY ○

Happy Full Moon, darling one. This month, the moon falls in the watery sign of Cancer. Cancer's ruling planet is the moon, which makes the energy a little more obvious, so you will feel it more. As the first Full Moon of 2023, there is a strong element to cleanse and purge anything that you are choosing to let go of and not carry into your year. What can you move through your body, flush through your body, clear from your home, cleanse from your space?

   Breathe and let go, that's it. Nurture yourself with this soft energy, with the gentleness and purity of a mother's love. Love your depths, your scars, your journey to now. Gently hold yourself and nourish all of you.

7 SATURDAY

8 SUNDAY

9 MONDAY

10 TUESDAY

Oshun's message for you – 'Today I am here in my body, present and fully aligned. I am allowing the sweetness of life, all that goodness and abundance, to come into my day and weave throughout my world.' Twirl that in.

11 WEDNESDAY

12 THURSDAY

13 FRIDAY

Your mission this weekend is to find, acquire, purchase or locate a journal. This journal will support you throughout the year, so choose one with a color, texture and feel that you love. Choose one that you are bursting to write in and fill with your story.

14 SATURDAY

15 SUNDAY ◑

16 MONDAY

Oshun's message for you – 'Today I allow myself to be loved more fully and completely by those around me. But most importantly, I choose to receive this love from myself. I'm learning that I am worthy of that.' Twirl that in through your body and throw your arms out to receive it.

17 TUESDAY

18 WEDNESDAY

19 THURSDAY

The dark night (before the New Moon tomorrow) is a wonderful opportunity for you to surrender. Surrender to what is in your life and to what isn't. This is a deep acceptance of your life now. Just breathe in and out, gently letting go and softening into your body.

20 FRIDAY

21 SATURDAY ●

As you stretch into your day, a beautiful and extra sparkly New Moon in the airy sign of Aquarius is beginning her cycle and shining her light into your life. You will find a beautiful meditation at www.niccigaraicoa.com/moonmeditations for you to harness the energy of the New Moon.

As the first New Moon for 2023, it's a beautiful opportunity for you to harness and feel into the dreams you would like to plant for this cycle of the moon (the next 29 days), and also your wider vision for the rest of your year. What feels possible and exciting for you in 2023?

22 SUNDAY

Happy Chinese New Year. 2023 is the year of the Water Rabbit, a lucky and fertile year for you. To bring in extra luck, wear something red today.

23 MONDAY

24 TUESDAY

Oshun's message for you – 'Today I notice the beauty of Goddess Oshun. I am learning that her beauty is simply a reflection of my own – for I am beautiful, too.' Twirl into your beauty.

25 WEDNESDAY

26 THURSDAY

Oshun's message for you – 'Today I allow the sacred gifts and talents that I was born with, the ones that I am here on Earth to use, the ones that make up and connect me to my magic – I allow them to come to the surface more and to nudge me with reminders when I forget who I am. I am learning how potent I am today.' Twirl that in through your body.

27 FRIDAY

28 SATURDAY ◐

29 SUNDAY

FEBRUARY

KUAN YIN

Your Moon Goddess for February is the loving Kuan Yin.

Kuan Yin is a Chinese Goddess of the Moon. She is very beautiful, with a small, delicate frame and loving eyes. She is wearing a traditional dress of white, gently embroidered with intricate patterns of ancient symbols of healing. She has her hair pinned up on her head and she wears a crown adorned with sacred crystals. She is standing, perfectly balanced, on a light pink lotus flower.

In her left hand, Kuan Yin is holding a large water jug, which contains sacred waters to cleanse away any pain and suffering that you are feeling. By cleansing yourself with the water, you can reach new levels of compassion and wisdom within. In her right hand, she is holding a willow branch. The willow branch signifies one's ability to be strong, yet flexible and hard to break.

Kuan Yin is the goddess of divine love, mercy and compassion. She can feel your pain, she can see your wounds, but she can also see your strength and the light that resides within you.

She has come through this month to support you to reach a new level of self-forgiveness and to help you participate in this ancient ritual of forgiveness and love with her. She is calling you to learn to love all the parts of yourself and your life so far.

Kuan Yin's mantra is 'I am learning how to be merciful, gentle and compassionate with myself.'

Her crystals are rose quartz, jade and aquamarine.

Her totem is the pink lotus flower in full bloom — to help you to feel divine and enlightened.

Her exercises are yoga, tai chi or qi gong — helping you to gently stretch into your body and into your day.

Her scents are rose, peony and lotus — for the blossoming of your life.

30 MONDAY

31 TUESDAY

Oshun's message for you – 'Today I decide that I deserve to be seen, that my words matter.
I am learning that I am enough, just as I am, in this very breath.' Twirl that in through your body.

I WEDNESDAY

2 THURSDAY

Place your hands on your heart and take five big breaths iiinnnnnnn and ouuuuuuut. From that lovely place of connection and love, go and be amazing you today.

3 FRIDAY

As the energy builds toward the Full Moon on Sunday, what do you need to use from your Goddess self-care toolkit to support you? Now do that!

4 SATURDAY

5 SUNDAY ○

Here is a Full Moon ritual for you to participate in as the moon reaches her fullness today.

Gather a pen, paper or your journal, as well as matches to light a candle or a safe fire, and begin to breathe with intention. Ask for your guides and Goddess Kuan Yin to come through to support you during this ritual.

Write down 10 things, stories or beliefs that you would like to clear the next layer of and burn away.

Read over your list and then safely light it on fire. As the paper burns, ask that the next layer is burned from your body and all levels known and unknown.

Breathe it out for at least 10 breaths.

Thank your guides, Kuan Yin, the moon and yourself for taking this sacred time for you. Take three big breaths and blow your candle out to close the space. Now go be amazing today.

6 MONDAY

7 TUESDAY

8 WEDNESDAY

9 THURSDAY

Kuan Yin's message for you – 'Today I choose to forgive
myself for the choices I made when I was younger and
didn't know any better.' Feel the petals of lotus flowers
float and twirl in and around your body, healing your next
layer of hurts and activating your divine potential just that
tiny bit more.

10 FRIDAY

11 SATURDAY

12 SUNDAY

13 MONDAY ◑

If you believed that you were worthy of receiving an extra four per cent of love today, I wonder what you might find sprinkled throughout your day? Keep your eyes open to receive it.

14 TUESDAY

Happy Love Day, sweetheart. Let's infuse your special day with radiant bubbles of love from Kuan Yin. What do you need to feel extra loved today? How can you give that to yourself? (Flowers are always lovely.)

15 WEDNESDAY

16 THURSDAY

As the moon gets smaller (waning) and the nights become darker, notice how your body feels in the morning and at night. Are you energized earlier or later in the day? Do you need to start going to bed earlier than usual? Are you sleeping in or waking early? It's kinda cool and interesting to notice what you are feeling with this moon phase. Self-discovery adventure time.

17 FRIDAY

18 SATURDAY

19 SUNDAY

The dark night before the New Moon is a time when you can take the opportunity to clear away anything that you have been holding onto, allowing it to flow away. It's a perfect day to declutter your space. Could you declutter just one drawer in your house or perhaps your desk today? I know you can and it will feel so lovely when it's done.

20 MONDAY

Happy New Moon, beautiful one! Today, you are greeted with a gorgeous New Moon in the watery sign of Pisces. It's all lighter today – creative, emotional, intuitive, spiritual, mystical and floaty.

Imagine that you are floating in the ocean, the waves are moving gently up and down, softly holding your body. You are held here, you are safe. Connect to the New Moon, feel her rays shining down onto your body, igniting healing, love and awareness. What is she whispering to you?

She is reminding you of your gifts, your talents, your magic.

Oh, and that you are a truly sacred part of this world.

You matter.

You are guided.

You belong.

Nawww, what a moon.

21 TUESDAY

22 WEDNESDAY

23 THURSDAY

Kuan Yin reminds you to use the power of your crystals today. Which crystal do you need? How will you use it? Why do you need it?

24 FRIDAY

25 SATURDAY

26 SUNDAY

Sunday is funday – how can you sprinkle some fun, play and pleasure into your day?

MARCH

ARIANRHOD

Your Moon Goddess for March is Arianrhod.

Arianrhod is a Celtic Goddess of the Moon. She is beautiful, pure and maiden-like, with skin white as snow, long wavy auburn hair and light pink lips. She wears a figure-hugging dress that skims and enhances her young body. She has earrings of dangly owl feathers that help her to tune into the wisdom of owl medicine.

From her left hand comes a silvery thread that forms a circle, a silvery wheel that Arianrhod uses to weave and create the tapestry of her life. She is often seen with a white wolf, who walks with her and signifies the power of the moon.

Arianrhod is the goddess of cycles — birth, death and karma. These cycles are both consistent and ever-changing throughout your life. Arianrhod gives you the courage to move through these times of change. She is your Moon Goddess for March because March is the time of the equinox, the time when the seasons change. She will bring you extra support through this time, as you learn to call in her medicine and weave your story, the tapestry of your life.

Arianrhod's mantra is 'I am learning how to stand in the light and love all parts of myself.'

Her crystals are moonstone, labradorite and selenite.

Her totems are owls, spinning wheels, birch trees and wolf medicine — tools that, for her, are the power of the moon.

Her exercises are any team sports that help you feel playful and part of a team.

Her scent is citrus: grapefruit, orange, lemon, lemon myrtle and verbena.

27 MONDAY ◑

Time to do your Goddess self-care toolkit for spring. Jump over to the page and let's get started!

28 TUESDAY

1 WEDNESDAY

Spend some time in nature this coming weekend to reset and reconnect to your own inner balance, your harmony.

2 THURSDAY

3 FRIDAY

Play your songs today from your Goddess self-care toolkit, sway those hips and jiggle out anything (energetic) that's not yours.

4 SATURDAY

5 SUNDAY

6 MONDAY

7 TUESDAY ○

The beautiful Grandmother Moon has turned that tiny bit more, claiming her total fullness as she lights up the sky with her brilliance. Today, she holds the space for you to feel into exactly what you need to clear, release, forgive and let go of during this potent time. She is illuminating those parts of your life that have stayed in the shadows or hidden from your sight, for a while.

She falls in the earthy sign of Virgo this month and she will guide you forward with grounded, aligned movements in the direction of your dreams. But move, you must. Tune into her whispers of guidance – she is sending them. Trust in her insights, trust in your intuition, trust in you. You are so ready for that extra nudge.

8 WEDNESDAY

9 THURSDAY

Arianrhod is sending you a disk of bright and sparkly silver thread. See it around your body, protecting you and helping you weave in your dreams, your life, your way.

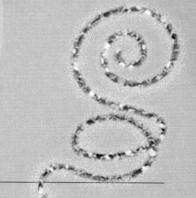

10 FRIDAY

11 SATURDAY

Gosh, what a beautiful day to be you! Throw those arms out and twirl into your weekend with extra joy.

12 SUNDAY

13 MONDAY

Just one more week to use all the tools you have chosen in your winter Goddess self-care toolkit. Dance, cook, smell, wear your crystal, call in your goddess and soak up those last fragments of support throughout your week.

14 TUESDAY

15 WEDNESDAY ◑

16 THURSDAY

17 FRIDAY

The dark nights of the waning moon are a time of such sacredness and magic. This lead-up to the New Moon birthing brings you this gift of beautiful, mystical nights, which hold the space for you to let go of anything you have been holding onto, allowing it to dissolve away. It's like a surrendering to all that is going on in your life right now, a softening into acceptance and love. A pause. How can you pause and rest more over this coming weekend?

18 SATURDAY

19 SUNDAY

Happy Mother's Day, UK! To all the moms who nurture and love their children, fur babies, family, friends, nieces, cousins and neighbors. Your love is so needed and valued. Thank you for your belief in the possibility and dreams of those around you. You change the world.

20 MONDAY

The Spring Equinox heralds the special day of equal parts day and night; the light and the shadow are balanced. This new light signifies balance, harmony, the shaking off of winter and the rebirth into your magical spring 2023.

   Stand outside (or where you can) for five minutes and allow these new rays of sunshine to penetrate through your body, aligning and balancing your whole presence to this new light. Receive the magic of this ancient celebration.

   Clear your space, declutter, wipe down the bench tops, clean the car and burn some incense to intentionally wipe away the winter cobwebs, creating the space to fill it with what you are choosing for spring.

21 TUESDAY ●

As you awaken and start to move your body, you are being illuminated with the flow of a beautiful New Moon in the fiery sign of Aries. The Aries New Moon starts the astrological cycle for the year. It's a fresh page – you get to choose what you would like to fill it with.

   You get to paint, draw or write all over your page with your desires, your dreams, your pleasure, your love. What do you want, darling one?

   Trust that you are being supported by your guides, by Arianrhod and by your angels. You are not alone. Allow love to guide and move you forward.

22 WEDNESDAY

23 THURSDAY

24 FRIDAY

And as if by magic, the wheel of the seasons turns, shifting the energy into the new delights of spring for you. Spring is the season of new beginnings, hope and expanding your energy out. You have rested this year through winter and, therefore, you are now strong and ready to bloom forth.

Spring is an exciting time where you are gently coming out to play, to socialize and to do the things you love. You have your self-care toolkit of support available and ready for you to use, so you will thrive through this season of rebirth. Ponder on what you love most about spring.

25 SATURDAY

26 SUNDAY

27 MONDAY

28 TUESDAY

29 WEDNESDAY ◐

Sprinkle the magic of your tools from this season into your week by making the space to know them and love them, even more.

30 THURSDAY

31 FRIDAY

Arianrhod's message for you is to ponder this: 'I know not, other than what I am.' How can you begin the journey of owning who you are today? Each tiny molecule of you has such an important job – they all link together to make you, you. Gosh, you're such a bad-ass!

1 SATURDAY

2 SUNDAY

MY GODDESS SELF-CARE TOOLKIT FOR SPRING

Spring is time to turn your focus outward. It's the phase of gently unfurling your leaves and rebirthing into this season. The weather is warming up, the days start to become longer and the flowers start to bloom.

Set your intentions for the next 12 weeks, which will be a time for you to see your magic and to sparkle brighter. This is also a great time for clearing clutter, a perfect time to wear some bright-colored clothing, a special time to journal, and a time for taking walks through nature and observing the changes happening all around you.

Have a look back at the toolkit you created for winter and note how it has supported you. Did you use all your tools to their full potential or does something need a little adjustment? Send each of your tools a big heartfelt thank you for supporting you through the last season.

You outgrow things that support you because you are always changing and growing and shifting. You will find yourself choosing different tools to support you for this season.

So, with tingles of excitement deep in your belly, let's get started!

All the self-care tools you choose here will support you from today until the Summer Solstice in June. These self-care tools will help you shine through your spring season with extra sprinkles of love and magic.

There are no right or wrong answers. Let go of your answers being any better, for they are all just your perfectly imperfect answers for today. Take five big breaths, really filling up your lungs, then let all your breath out. Imagine a slippery dip is going from your thinking mind into your heart space. Feel yourself sliding down and landing in your heart. Open your heart space a little wider (even if you are unsure if you're doing it right, trust that you are) – that's it!

GODDESS

Let's start with choosing a goddess. Flip through until you come to April, May and June. Really notice the picture of each goddess and read the description about her. Which goddess feels like she will help you the most this season?

The goddess I have chosen to support me throughout spring 2023 is

_____

She will support me with the medicine of her

_____

COLOR

Choose one color that is going to support you throughout spring. Land on your color and write it down here:

_____

When I see this color, I feel

_____

I can use this color to support me throughout spring with things such as clothing, accessories, jewelry, flowers, scatter cushions, candles, crystals, pens and

_____

SONGS

Choose three upbeat songs. Songs that you love, songs that get you up and moving, songs that make you feel it's impossible to stay completely still, songs that make you feel like you want to boom-shakka-lakka and shimmy-shake around your house.

When you feel irritated, what could you do to get those deep irritations and emotions out of your body? You can dance them out! Yes, I know it sounds a little bit weird (okay, super weird) but it really does work.

If I am feeling a little triggered, angry, scared, irritated or just in a funk, I play these three songs so I can get all loose and not caring, and allow the music and dance to move me through the emotion.

My three songs are:

1. _____

2. _____

3. _____

Your song mission is to download your three songs and create a special spring playlist on your phone so that, whenever you need them, they are ready for you.

EXERCISE

Don't moan when you read the word 'exercise'. It will be okay, I promise. Moving your body is important: you know that, I know that, everyone knows that. If there was a magical place that you could visit and it would transform your body with the push of a button, we'd all go there, right? Unfortunately, I am yet to discover this place so, for now, we all have to move our bodies to keep them strong and bendy in the ways we have available to us at this moment.

Make this exercise as joyful, pleasurable, enlightening and as fun as it can be. There are so many ways to move your body. Choose one that feels exciting for you now.

The ways I will move my body during spring are:

_____

I will do these at _____ (location), _____ times per week.

FRAGRANCE

Your nose is a powerful tool. When you smell something you love, your whole body can feel so happy. It is like your nose holds this secret power to connect you to what brings you pleasure. You even have memories triggered by your sense of smell. In choosing to notice these scents you love, and by sprinkling them throughout your day, you will trigger a pleasure response that reminds you to feel all loved up and amazing. Kinda cool, hey!

For spring, choose one smell that is going to support you through this season. It could be an essential oil, a perfume, a flower. Choose something you just love, that is easy to use and fills you with pleasure.

Land on your fragrance and write it down here:

_____

When your nostrils are tickled with this fragrance, how do you feel?

_____

I can use this fragrance as my signature spring scent to support me in lots of ways, such as burning essential oils and candles, using in skincare, eating or cooking with it, wearing the perfume, smelling fresh flowers, as well as

_____ and _____

CRYSTALS

Crystals are like magical particles that hold healing powers within. There are thousands of crystals available and they all have individual characteristics or ways to support you. Using the magic of one crystal helps to guide you with what you are working on, with healing, clearing or reminding you how you are growing and what you are wanting to step into.

The crystal I am choosing to support me for spring is called

_____

It is _____ (color) and it will help me to _____

I can use this crystal to support me in lots of ways, such as carrying a piece in my pocket, or keeping a piece in the car or my bag. I could wear it in jewelry, use it as a screensaver on my phone, pop it under my pillow or mattress to support me while I sleep or I could

_____ or _____

MANTRA

By now, you know what you are working on and how you would like to feel. Have a look at the goddesses from April, May and June. Choose one of the mantras they have sent to you.

I am learning how to

_____

Your special mantra mission is to write your affirmation on post-it notes and sprinkle these words around your home, work office, phone and car. Write it down every week in this diary until the Summer Solstice to remind you to say it. Write it in lipstick on your mirror or in your journal, or perhaps you could

_____

For an extra gold star for being amazing, fill in three things you love most about spring.

1._____

2._____

3._____

I will choose to do these things more because they bring me pleasure and fill my heart with joy. I deserve joy. (Yes, you really do!)

Well done. That is your very own Goddess self-care toolkit for spring all finished and completed. It will be here to support you through to the Summer Solstice in June.

Call in your goddess and play your three boppy songs now, swaying those hips as you dance and twirl around in celebration of completing your toolkit.

April

ISIS

Your Moon Goddess for April is Isis.

Isis is an Egyptian Goddess of the Moon. She is very powerful, strong and beautiful, with a delicate frame and loving eyes. She is wearing a long Egyptian embroidered dress and she wears a wesekh — an intricately beaded neckpiece — draped around her neck and chest with intricate patterns of ancient symbols of healing. Isis's hair is falling loosely to her neck, and she wears a gorgeous crown of gold adorned with cow horns with a disk held between them, symbolizing the sun. In her hands, she is holding a crescent moon, her favorite time of the moon cycle.

Isis is the goddess of the Divine Mother, of fertility, magic, love, change and healing. She has come through this month to support you to feel your deepest desires and help you to give birth to these dreams. With the power of the sacred waters, she brings you healing so you may clear what is in your past that holds you back from your dreams.

Isis sends you the magic of believing that your dreams matter and so you may experience a new form of loving yourself with her waves of magical, loving light.

Isis's mantra is 'I am learning to choose my dreams first.'

Her crystals are lapis lazuli and Isis quartz.

Her totems are falcon feathers and the traditional Egyptian symbol called the ankh, the key of life.

Her exercises are walking and running — great ways to keep your body moving.

Her scents are frankincense, myrrh and vetiver — beautiful smells that connect her to higher truths.

3 MONDAY

Isis sends you a cloak of falcon feathers to drape across your shoulders. This cloak is to keep you safe, protected and held, as you begin the journey of choosing to live your dreams. Can you feel it on your shoulders?

4 TUESDAY

5 WEDNESDAY

6 THURSDAY ○

Today, the moon turned that tiny bit more, stretching into her fullness and shining her glow throughout your world. Today, she falls in the airy sign of Libra. Libra is balance; this really powerful moon is shining her light down so you notice, so you can release and heal the next small part of your life that needs attention. So you may uncover what you need to have a more balanced life for the rest of 2023.

Sometimes, it is uncomfortable and annoying and scary to face the music of your life, but should you doubt yourself and your abilities right now, you simply need to look up. Grandmother Moon and Isis are both there for you.

7 FRIDAY

8 SATURDAY

9 SUNDAY

Today opens a beautiful Easter healing gateway of transformation for you. Imagine that a waterfall of light and love is cascading down, through and around your whole body, lighting you up from within. You are so loved and held in this healing energy, receive it with open arms and twirl around in it.

10 MONDAY

11 TUESDAY

12 WEDNESDAY

What needs your attention this week? 'Everything' is too overwhelming, just pick one priority and move with that. Strutting in that direction helps, too.

13 THURSDAY ◑

14 FRIDAY

15 SATURDAY

16 SUNDAY

17 MONDAY

In the lead-up to the solar eclipse on Thursday, you will find yourself getting a little stirred up, out of sorts or feeling argumentative, tired or irritated. Be gentle with yourself and those around you during this time. Your awareness of what is going on for you is key – use your Goddess self-care toolkit to support you.

18 TUESDAY

19 WEDNESDAY

The dark night, before the New Moon tomorrow, brings you the opportunity to take one last pause. Feeling really tired is normal around this time in the moon cycle. Have you noticed that? Does your bedtime need adjusting tonight? It's a great time for an easy dinner, clearing off your bedside table, and having extra water, essential oil and snuggles in bed with a person, pillow, animal or teddy. What do you need?

20 THURSDAY

The energy of this second Aries New Moon, mixed with the solar eclipse, feels a little unsettling, tiresome and different to 'normal'. A solar eclipse is where the moon covers the sun and darkens its surface, intensifying the depth of what is coming into your awareness.

What are you feeling? With a sense of wonder and curiosity, notice what is coming up in your life right now. What emotions are surfacing? Where are you feeling stuck? What thoughts are on repeat? What are your dreams trying to communicate? What adventures are calling to your heart? What is the big obstacle that feels in your way?

Don't place a judgment on anything you might discover. Choose to notice, to journal on it and to learn more about yourself. You're so worthy of that.

21 FRIDAY

22 SATURDAY

You are still aligning and feeling into the shifts from the New Moon and solar eclipse. What do you need from your Goddess self-care toolkit to support you this weekend?

23 SUNDAY

24 MONDAY

You can have your dreams. 'I am learning to actively create the life I choose, one baby step at a time.' Isis sends you this wonderful daily affirmation to support you this week.

25 TUESDAY

26 WEDNESDAY

27 THURSDAY ◖

28 FRIDAY

Isis sends you this sacred mantra: 'Today, I accept that I am born into this world with a long list of my very own sacred gifts, they are enough in every way. I choose to see them more. I choose to see them reflected back at me throughout my day. I choose to own them as enough. I choose to own me as enough.' Such powerful healing here for you; breathe it into your body.

29 SATURDAY

30 SUNDAY

MAMA QUILLA

Your Moon Goddess for May is Mama Quilla.

Mama Quilla is an Incan Goddess, known as 'Mother Moon'. Mama Quilla is exceptionally beautiful, with brown skin and long dark hair with whispers of silvery gray shining through. She has a strong frame and a sense of fierceness about her. She is wearing a traditional dress and long cape, both embroidered lovingly with sacred symbols from the Inca period.

On her head, she is wearing a large half-circle crown of silver, with the phases of the moon etched in and encrusted with jewels. She cries tears of silver, which flow down her face. She is standing with the moon in a partial lunar eclipse, and so she stands in the shadows.

In Inca times, she was known as the defender of women. She was a powerhouse of strength and deeply held wisdom. Priestesses of this time would serve and worship her in temples that were dedicated to her wisdom and beauty. She is the ruler of marriage, menstrual cycles and childbirth, and is the protector of women in all areas.

On lunar eclipses, the Incas would fear that an animal was attacking Mama Quilla. They would hold ceremonies that would scare away the animal so that light would be restored once again throughout their world. It feels appropriate to have her as our May goddess because there is a lunar eclipse this month.

Mama Quilla is the goddess of being fierce and divinely feminine. She oozes strength, poise and grace. She has come through this month to support you in connecting to the natural phases and cycles of your body, the moon, nature and the seasons, and to help you restore balance, harmony and the beautiful flow of the divine feminine within you.

Mama Quilla's mantra is 'I am learning to flow with the sacred cycles of my body, of nature and of the moon, to fiercely claim my femininity and my potency'.

Her crystals are opals, rubies, silver and garnets.

Her totems are hand-made earthen pieces such as tapestries, woven cloth, clay bowls and pottery cups, and her animal is the crow.

Her exercises are power-lifting and strength training — exercises that support building muscle and a strong body.

Her scents are those that strengthen your confidence such as black pepper, ginger, lemongrass, coriander and lemon.

I MONDAY

The beautiful space between eclipses allows you to feel into what you want, but it's also a time when you may find a big-ass spotlight shining its radiant beam on your crap. It's rather obvious and uncomfortable, and can feel really irritating.

It's like you can now see from a new perspective all the hurts that you thought were neatly tucked away or buried deep inside. They all bubble up to the surface, so you can choose whether to carry them anymore. As you move through this time, awareness, forgiveness, compassion and being gentle with yourself is just so important. What can you use from your Goddess self-care toolkit to support you this week? Dancing out irritations is always fun.

2 TUESDAY

3 WEDNESDAY

4 THURSDAY

The lead-up to the lunar eclipse tomorrow feels a little uncomfortable or extra irritating. But you have a secret weapon this month, you have Mama Quilla to help you. Imagine that she is crying tears of silver, which are flowing down from her eyes all through your body to hold you with her potent and unconditional love.

5 FRIDAY ○

Happy Full Moon Lunar Eclipse Day to you! It's such a climactic day of big shifts, changes, breaking free and 'seeing' what has been hidden from you, perhaps for a long time. This month, she falls in the watery sign of Scorpio, so you may be feeling really emotional and like old wounds are resurfacing to be cleared, especially wounds of the heart. Allow the tears to fall and release.

It's such a wonderful moon to sit, meditate or journal under, allowing yourself the time to connect into the deep wisdom available to you.

6 SATURDAY

7 SUNDAY

8 MONDAY

9 TUESDAY

Mama Quilla asks you: 'How can you give to yourself, love yourself, trust yourself even more passionately during this moment and through your day?'

10 WEDNESDAY

11 THURSDAY

To reset the cycles in your body, are you brave enough to try immersing your whole body in some water – the ocean, a lake, a pool, or your bathtub or shower? Call in and ask to connect to Mama Quilla and the moon, don't overthink it, just trust you've got this – and allow the water to flow over you, cleansing your body and resetting all of the cycles in your whole physical body. Give it a go!

12 FRIDAY ◑

13 SATURDAY

14 SUNDAY

Happy Mother's Day, America! To all the moms who nurture and love their children, fur babies, family, friends, nieces, cousins and neighbors. Your love is so needed and valued. Thank you for your belief in the possibility and dreams of those around you. You change the world.

15 MONDAY

16 TUESDAY

I am trusting that I am making progress. My fierce and brave baby steps all add up, and they move me in the direction of my dreams. I'm pretty awesome!

17 WEDNESDAY

18 THURSDAY

Tonight's dark night brings you the opportunity to take a last pause before the New Moon begins tomorrow. Feeling extra tired is normal around this time in the moon cycle. What do you need to support you from your toolkit? Extra cuddles are always lovely, too.

19 FRIDAY

Today brings you a Black Moon in the earthy sign of Taurus. It's a time of new beginnings and a wonderful time for you to start feeling into what you would like to achieve this month. This New Moon energy will inspire you to take the time to ponder your wishes and intentions, getting a clearer picture of your hopes and dreams.

It's an expansive time with vast possibilities, so much more is possible for you now. Keep it simple, achievable, fun, sensual ... dreams that feel pleasurable and attainable. Feel into that, using your intuition, for it is heightened under this moon.

There is great power to be found in being honest and vulnerable under this moon.

20 SATURDAY

21 SUNDAY

22 MONDAY

_____

23 TUESDAY

_____

24 WEDNESDAY

_____

25 THURSDAY

Mama Quilla says: 'Paint the picture of your life with the blinkers removed, with simplicity, play, a sense of connection and respect to Mother Earth, sustainability, oneness and love ... deeply honoring yourself. That way, you always feel more fabulous and more unapologetically you.'

26 FRIDAY

27 SATURDAY ◑

28 SUNDAY

Dancing under the moon to your songs will really turn up your pleasure factor – try it!

JUNE

ARCHANGEL HANIEL

Your Moon Goddess for June is Archangel Haniel.

While not traditionally defined as a Goddess, I think Archangel Haniel, as an archangel, deserves this title and she really wanted to come through this month to support you.

Archangel Haniel is one of the seven recognized archangels in Jewish and Christian faiths, so for them, she is honored as a Goddess of the Moon. Archangel Haniel is beautiful, with pale skin and golden hair. She has gray loving eyes and is wearing an angelic dress of blush pink that matches perfectly with her huge and amazing angel wings.

Archangel Haniel has an incredibly strong connection to her intuition and her third eye chakra. She strengthens and activates her gifts of insight and wisdom daily, so she remains in a balanced state of flow with her connection to the divine.

She stands radiantly, confidently and with elegance, held in the gentle power of the moon's glow lighting her way.

Between her hands radiates a ball of turquoise light, signifying the water of the sea.

Archangel Haniel is the archangel of intuition, divine wisdom, magic and truth. She has come through this month to help you access your intuitive gifts and to symbolize the bridge between the realms, linking you to the truth — and the magic — of who you truly are.

Archangel Haniel's mantra is 'I am learning how to trust that I am supported by my guides.'

Her crystals are moonstone, opal and clear quartz.

Her totems are feathers and pictures in the clouds — signs that float into your life to remind you that you are supported.

Her exercises are yoga, barre, pilates — exercises that keep your core strong.

Her scents are soft and gentle ones, such as ylang-ylang, lavender and chamomile.

29 MONDAY

30 TUESDAY

31 WEDNESDAY

1 THURSDAY

2 FRIDAY

Archangel Haniel's mantra for you this coming weekend is: 'I trust that I am being supported by my guides, by the universe, by my angels. I am not alone and I allow love to guide and move me forward.' Awhhhhh, yeah, you do.

3 SATURDAY

4 SUNDAY ○

Happy Full Moon, beautiful one. Today, she falls in the fiery sign of Sagittarius, the sign of passion, adventure and doing things your way. You may be feeling fired up about something, angry, powerless, discontented or just sick of dragging baggage around with you.

Allow your tears to fall as part of your release process – that is so healing.

Journal on what are you being called to 'let go of', so you may step into the empowered version of yourself for the rest of 2023. You deserve your dreams, those wild and free ones, this year.

Choose. Them.

5 MONDAY

6 TUESDAY

If you looked back on what you have achieved during spring what would you notice? Can you see what you have accomplished? Write it down so you can be reminded of what you have done well. Celebrate your success and your amazingness by doing something special for yourself. What will you do, or buy, or how could you treat yourself?

7 WEDNESDAY

8 THURSDAY

Just a few days left, before the Summer Solstice, to use your spring self-care toolkit, squeezing and soaking up those last fragments of support. Play your songs, wear your color, smell your fragrance, move your body and use your crystal energy as much as you can to turn up receiving support. Bathe in the delicious support you have.

9 FRIDAY

10 SATURDAY ◑

11 SUNDAY

12 MONDAY

If you walked to the beat of your own drum, to the music of your heart, to the sound of your soul ... how would your life look? What would be different? How would it be different to your life now? What are you dreaming of that fills your soul and body with a sense of lightness, play and pleasure? What gives you hope? Taking the time to discern what you want before the Summer Solstice will really support you. Journal on this and be open to seeing what you discover, as you sit in a place of deep introspection.

13 TUESDAY

14 WEDNESDAY

Archangel Haniel is sending you your very own sacred ball of turquoise light to place in your heart. This light will sit here in your heart space for the rest of spring, supporting you to light up from within and to see the truth of who you are reflected back at you throughout your day.

15 THURSDAY

16 FRIDAY

17 SATURDAY

The dark nights before the New Moon bring you the opportunity to take one last pause. It's where you get to clear and release anything you may have been holding onto, or to clear away any clutter that remains. Remember, feeling tired is normal around this time in the moon cycle. What do you need today to feel nurtured and loved? How can you ask for that or give it to yourself?

18 SUNDAY ●

New Moon beginnings are yours today. Feel the flow of this and pull it down into your body. This month, she falls in the airy sign of Gemini, the sign of the mind and your intellect. Stay open to new intuitive insights and wisdom flowing through with this moon. Listen to your world closely to hear what is being repeated to you: songs, words, feathers, etc. What do you need inspiration and support with? If you had the courage to ask for what you want right now, what would that be?

Dare to dream bigger and wider.

PS: Happy Fathers Day to all the dads out there who fill the world with their love.

19 MONDAY

20 TUESDAY

The wheel of the seasons turns, shifting the energy into summer, the season of adventure, getting social, allowing the sun to recharge your body and expanding your energy out further than what you did in spring.

Summer is an exciting time where you are really connecting to what brings you joy and pleasure, doing the things you love with the people you love to be around. You have your Goddess self-care toolkit of support available and ready for you to use, so you will thrive through this season of vitality.

What do you love most about summer? How can you do more of that this year?

21 WEDNESDAY

Today marks the beautiful Summer Solstice, a day that begins the new cycle of the sun's potent energy. It's the longest day of the year and a chance to really connect to the life force of the sun as it reaches its highest point in the sky.

The energy of summer will start to intensify; nature expands, growth is at its best and most vibrant capacity because its vital focus is expanding outward and filling the world with joy. It's a beautiful time to shine your light on your own life as you step into your more. Take the moment to reconnect to your life force and passions, grounding deeply into this day and lighting up from within!

Meditate, connect to nature, go within, find your stillness and allow the blessings of this time to shower down upon you. See the seeds of your dreams being lovingly held and nurtured into life by the earth. Breathe in deeply and fill your body with hope, trust and stillness.

Stay on the lookout for fairies, because this was the day in ancient times that fairies would show themselves to humans!

22 THURSDAY

23 FRIDAY

24 SATURDAY

25 SUNDAY

There is a lot of energy brewing and stirring
at this time – remember that if you didn't
feel the nudge, you wouldn't know that you
are ready for change ... trust in the nudge.

26 MONDAY ◐

_____

27 TUESDAY

_____

28 WEDNESDAY

_____

29 THURSDAY

Time to do your new Goddess self-care toolkit – jump over now and let's do this!

30 FRIDAY

1 SATURDAY

2 SUNDAY

MY GODDESS SELF-CARE TOOLKIT FOR SUMMER

Summer is the time for expanding your energy outward, catching up with friends, feeling the sun's rays on your body, spreading your joy and magic through your world.

Set your intentions for the next 12 weeks, which will be a time for you to honor your space, set your boundaries, and a great time for choosing your pleasure. This is a time for summer love, toes in the sand, barbecues, picnics and ocean swims.

Have a look back at the toolkit you created for spring and note how it has supported you. Did you use all of your tools to their full potential or does something need a little adjustment? Send each of your tools a big heartfelt thank you for supporting you through the last season.

You outgrow things that support you because you are always changing and growing and shifting. You will find yourself choosing different tools to support you for this season. So, with tingles of excitement deep in your belly, let's get started!

All the self-care tools you choose here will support you from today until the Fall Equinox at the end of September. These self-care tools will help you shine through your summer season with extra sprinkles of love and magic.

There are no right or wrong answers. Let go of your answers being any better, for they are all just your perfectly imperfect answers for today. Take five big breaths, really filling up your lungs, then let all your breath out. Imagine a slippery dip is going from your thinking mind into your heart space. Feel yourself sliding down and landing in your heart. Open your heart space a little wider (even if you are unsure if you're doing it right, trust that you are) – that's it!

GODDESS

Let's start with choosing a goddess. Flip through until you come to July, August and September.

Really notice the picture of each goddess and read the description about her. Which goddess feels like she will help you the most this season?

The goddess I have chosen to support me throughout summer 2023 is

_____

She will support me with the medicine of her

_____

COLOR

Choose one color that is going to support you throughout summer. Land on your color and write it down here:

_____

When I see this color, I feel

_____

I can use this color to support me throughout summer with things such as clothing, accessories, jewelry, flowers, scatter cushions, candles, crystals, pens and

_____

SONGS

Choose three upbeat songs. Songs that you love, songs that get you up and moving, songs that make you feel that it's impossible to stay completely still, songs that make you feel like you want to boom-shakka-lakka and shimmy-shake around your house.

When you feel irritated, what could you do to get those deep irritations and emotions out of your body? You can dance them out! Yes, I know it sounds a little bit weird (okay, super weird) but it really does work.

If I am feeling a little triggered, angry, scared, irritated or just in a funk, I can play these three songs so I can get all loose and not caring, and allow the music and dance to move me through the emotion.

My three songs are:

1. _____

2. _____

3. _____

Your song mission is to download your three songs and create a special summer playlist on your phone so that, whenever you need them, they are ready for you.

EXERCISE

Don't moan when you read the word 'exercise'. It will be okay, I promise. Moving your body is important: you know that, I know that, everyone knows that. If there was a magical place that you could visit and it would transform your body with the push of a button, we'd all go there, right? Unfortunately, I am yet to discover this place so, for now, we all have to move our bodies to keep them strong and bendy, in the ways we have available to us at this moment.

Make this exercise as joyful, pleasurable, enlightening and as fun as it can be. There are so many ways to move your body. Choose one that feels exciting for you now.

The ways I will move my body during summer are:

_____

I will do these at _____ (location), _____ times per week.

FRAGRANCE

Your nose is a powerful tool. When you smell something you love, your whole body can feel so happy. It is like your nose holds this secret power to connect you to what brings you pleasure. You even have memories triggered by your sense of smell. In choosing to notice these scents you love, and by sprinkling them throughout your day, you will trigger a pleasure response that reminds you to feel all loved up and amazing. Kinda cool, hey!

For summer, choose one smell that is going to support you throughout this season. It could be an essential oil, a perfume, a flower. Choose something you just love, that is easy to use and fills you with pleasure.

Land on your fragrance and write it down here:

_____

I can use this fragrance as my signature summer scent to support me in lots of ways, such as burning essential oils and candles, using in skincare, eating or cooking with it, wearing the perfume, smelling fresh flowers, as well as

_____ and _____

When your nostrils are tickled with this fragrance, how do you feel?

_____

CRYSTALS

Crystals are like magical particles that hold healing powers within. There are thousands of crystals available and they all have individual characteristics or ways to support you. Using the magic of one crystal helps to guide you with what you are working on, with healing, clearing energy or reminding you how you are growing and what you are wanting to step into.

The crystal I am choosing to support me for summer is called

_____

It is _____ (color) and it will help me to _____

I can use this crystal to support me in lots of ways, such as carrying a piece in my pocket, or keeping a piece in the car or my bag. I could wear it in jewelry, use it as a screensaver on my phone, pop it under my pillow or mattress to support me while I sleep, or I could

_____ or

MANTRA

You know what you are working on and how you would like to feel. Have a look at the goddesses from July, August and September. Choose one of the mantras they have sent to you.

I am learning how to

_____

Your special mantra mission is to write your affirmation on post-it notes and sprinkle these words around your home, work office, phone and car. Write it down every week in this diary until the Fall Equinox to remind you to say it. Record your voice saying this affirmation now, then again in September and notice the difference. Write it in lipstick on your mirror or in your journal, or perhaps you could

_____

For an extra gold star for being amazing, fill in three things you love most about summer.

1. _____

2. _____

3. _____

July

IX CHEL

Your Moon Goddess for July is Ix Chel (pronounced Ischel).

Ix Chel is a Mayan Goddess of the Moon. She is an older woman with wise, loving eyes, wrinkles, and is wearing a traditional Mayan brightly colored, woven skirt. Her gray, wispy hair is pinned up on her head and she wears a serpent as a crown. She is sitting on a waning moon. Ix Chel loves wearing colorful jewelry that she makes from gifts she's collected from the land where she lives.

In her hands, she is holding a ceramic jug filled with water, which she pours over your whole body to clear and cleanse you with its sacred waters from her homeland.

Ix Chel is the goddess of love, medicine, creativity, the arts and childbirth — she wants you to feel what it is like to love fully and completely, to create magic with your hands, how to nurture yourself with the medicine of Mother Earth, and to procreate and give birth to your pleasure and joy.

Ix Chel's mantra is 'I am learning how creative I am when I play. I easily make magic with my hands.'

Her crystals are petrified wood, tiger's eye, granite, clay, shells and fossils.

Her totems are snakes for transformation and a woven basket for collecting things from nature.

Her exercises are swimming in the ocean, hiking, bushwalking — ways to immerse yourself in Mother Nature and to feel inspired.

Her scents are earthy, such as pine, eucalyptus, sandalwood and cedarwood.

3 MONDAY ◯

As you wake into your day, a gorgeous Full Moon in Capricorn is nudging you to stand in your strength and power, clearing away the next layer of anything that doesn't allow you to do this.

The angelic realm and your spirit guides are calling you to connect to the support they offer you through this uncomfortable time. They are there. The earth wisdom of Gaia – Mother Nature – is invoking you to connect with her by grounding deep into the healing from the earth.

You have access to this glorious time where the whole universe is conspiring for your greatest outcome. It's loving you deeply into your greatest potential.

Today, you belong. Just as you are. Ix Chel knows this to be true.

4 TUESDAY

What would you like to write a declaration of independence from? An emotion, a person, a habit, a belief perhaps that is holding you back? Where are you feeling the need to be free in your life right now?

I (insert name)_____ am claiming independance from _____
on the 4th July 2023. I stand proudly here today, empowered and in a state of flow and grace as I learn how to support myself even more this month. Twirl or dance that in.

5 WEDNESDAY

6 THURSDAY

7 FRIDAY

Use your Goddess self-care toolkit this coming weekend – play, create, sing, wander and smell those fragrances.

8 SATURDAY

9 SUNDAY

10 MONDAY

Goddess Ix Chel invites you to sit in stillness as she pours over you the healing waters from her ceramic jug. Feel them flow down into your body, clearing and cleansing, in exactly the way you need them most from her today.

11 TUESDAY

12 WEDNESDAY

How can you create magic with your hands through your week? Cooking, creating, dancing, crafts, art, cuddling, kissing, caressing ... these are all ways you create magic in your life. What will you choose?

13 THURSDAY

14 FRIDAY

The moon is starting to get smaller and less bright and sparkly in her waning way. This is when you finish projects; have earlier meetings; declutter your home, car and office; and where you may just need to climb into bed early. What do you need this coming weekend?

15 SATURDAY

16 SUNDAY

The dark night before this New Moon brings you the opportunity to take a last pause before the New Moon begins tomorrow. It's where you get to clear and release anything you may have been holding onto, or to clear away any clutter that remains. Remember, feeling really tired is normal around this time in the moon cycle. What do you need today to feel held during this time? How can you ask for that or give it to yourself?

17 MONDAY ●

Out of the darkness and the rest, she turns that tiny, smidgy bit more and is reborn today into her new cycle. It's a wonderful New Moon in the watery sign of Cancer.

With the moon in Cancer, you will notice a need to fill your cup first, so consistent self-love will be a priority. Cancer is such a deeply feminine sign. It's the divine feminine and divine mother, the sign of family and home. Use this energy to 'feel' and 'listen' to what you need, to stay aligned, balanced, calm and supported.

Expand into this divine energy, throw your arms out with gratitude, knowing how supported you are right now and grounded in those New Moon intentions, so you don't get washed away with the energy and you remain strong.

18 TUESDAY

19 WEDNESDAY

20 THURSDAY

Skinny dipping, rope swings, creeks, beach strolls, sunsets over the water, baths filled with bubbles and flower petals, mermaiding, sparkling water with fresh lime, pool swims, rain dancing, waterfalls – so, so many fun ways to be around water. Which one will you choose to support you?

21 FRIDAY

22 SATURDAY

23 SUNDAY

24 MONDAY

Ix Chel is sending you snake medicine from the serpent she wears on her head. This snake medicine is winding through your inner core (kundalini) to transform and heal your energetic systems, or chakras. Breathe it up and feel into this shift.

25 TUESDAY ◑

26 WEDNESDAY

27 THURSDAY

28 FRIDAY

Ix Chel directs you to find something from nature this week that reminds you of the beauty of the summer season: a feather, a flower, a fallen leaf, a butterfly wing or a seed pod, then stick it in your diary or create something with it. Find something from around where you live, work or play, so you are bringing in the medicine from your environment.

29 SATURDAY

30 SUNDAY

AUGUST

LUNA

Your Moon Goddess for August is Luna.

Luna is a Roman Goddess of the Moon. She is ethereal, charming, sexy, feminine and beautiful, with brown hair, amber eyes and soft brown skin. She is wearing a cream-colored traditional Roman dress with gold braid around her waist and breasts. She embodies the moon and its cycles, so she wears a crown adorned with moon symbols and sacred jewels to remind her of her potent power.

Luna is the goddess of fertility, intuition and dreams. She has come through this month so she can help you give birth to your dreams and desires, sending you inspiration and insights while you sleep or meditate.

Luna's mantra is 'I am learning that, as I soften and surrender, I am deeply connected to support my intuition.'

Her crystals are moonstone, larimar and super seven.

Her totem is the sign of the triple goddess: the combination of maiden, mother and wise woman.

Her exercises are swimming, stand-up paddle boarding, surfing and fire twirling.

Her scents are herbaceous scents such as basil, thyme, rosemary and mint, using these beautiful garden herbs to heal you from the inside.

31 MONDAY

Can you feel something brewing? Are you feeling affected by the moon energy as she builds up to her fullness? She will be showering you with love, support and guidance, as she does each night, but sometimes you can feel irritated, have lots of lucid dreams, be triggered in some way – especially during Super Moons. They are super strong and closer to Earth, so you can feel them more. What do you need from your Goddess self-care toolkit to support you through the next few days?

1 TUESDAY ○

Happy first Full Moon for August, beautiful one! Today, she falls in the airy sign of Aquarius. Aquarius energy is expansive, intuitive, humanitarian – working toward better outcomes for all – it's dreamy and filled with hope. It's a time for you to dream.

Aquarius energy is also really good at bringing up stories of times when you couldn't get what you wanted. It's a time when you can get caught up in other people's dreams or expectations for your life. Staying grounded in your body will support you to stay strong. You have such a potent amount of tools to help you during this moon; remember to use your Goddess self-care toolkit!

2 WEDNESDAY

3 THURSDAY

4 FRIDAY

Trust that Goddess Luna is there to support you and your dreams. Could you let go a little more and surrender to what is today? Can you really trust her and allow her to lead you? Can you relax and be, knowing that she *is* guiding you to be you, but more 'you' than you have perhaps allowed yourself to be before? What a powerful ally you have.

5 SATURDAY

This beautiful energy from the Super Moon on the 1st will link you into the Lions Gate portal, a healing gateway that is open now and will continue to grow to its most potent day on the 8th of August 8:8, the infinity sign doubled.

6 SUNDAY

7 MONDAY

The Lions Gate portal of 2023 is continuing to build and grow in strength and intensity. It's a beautiful time to sit in meditation, allowing your heart to be opened and connect into your intuition more. The veil between dimensions is so thin, be open to Goddess Luna and your guides sending you support. Allow their wisdom to rain down on your soul and connect firmly into your heart, into your feet and into the path that you are walking. What is your intention for this portal?

8 TUESDAY ◑

The Lions Gate portal of 2023 has reached its most potent and powerful day. It remains open until the 12th of August, when it closes for the year. This gateway is a really sacred time that has been honored and celebrated for many thousands of years, especially by ancient civilizations. It occurs when the sun, the Earth and the star Sirius move to specific points in the sky.

Feeling tired, a little emotional – out of sorts? These are all side effects of this portal. Relax and take the time to rest and recalibrate over the next four days, so you can take advantage of all that goodness, boldness and lion courage being sent your way.

9 WEDNESDAY

10 THURSDAY

The Lions Gate portal has been so massive this year. Did you feel any shifts, intuitive insights or wisdom come through for you? What have you noticed? There are two days left to take advantage of this gateway for 2023.

How can Luna support you to feel ready for your next baby steps forward? What do you need?

What color could you choose to remind you to be courageous, calm and ready to lead yourself forward in the direction of your dreams?

What do you need from your Goddess self-care toolkit to take full advantage of this sacred and supportive energy?

11 FRIDAY

12 SATURDAY

13 SUNDAY

14 MONDAY

15 TUESDAY

For today, the day before a New Moon, the last day of the moon cycle, as the darkness flows in, you have some really beautiful things to do … Today is where you can really use the darkness of the sky to clear, clean, smudge your house, let go of things, declutter your space. Inviting any last things that you need to let go of before the New Moon begins tomorrow to come into your awareness.

You may be feeling tired. It's not the easiest time to push yourself with high physical exertions or high-pressure situations. Rest and take one last pause before the new cycle begins tomorrow, honoring your journey so far on this moon cycle and reflecting on just how far you have grown into you, more.

16 WEDNESDAY ●

Today, you will wake into your day, stretching into a beautiful New Moon in Leo, firing you up and igniting your potency. Can you feel that glorious shift? Stretch and spin around, twirling into your connection to this New Moon.

It's time to infuse more of your desires into your life. Get creative with these: find the joy, the playfulness, the fun, and how they can be more infused into your week. Fire up, baby, this is going to be an exciting month for you.

17 THURSDAY

Can you spot the moon tonight? Imagine that Luna is sitting on the moon, sending you moonbeams and love and inspiration while you sleep.

18 FRIDAY

19 SATURDAY

20 SUNDAY

Today, immerse yourself in the healing powers of Mother Earth. Allow all the earthly goodness to hold and support you. Look around, really see all the ways that the elements teach, play, be and work to balance and support you ... it's all there just for you; choose to notice.

21 MONDAY

As August draws to a close, look back on your year and notice the ways you have connected to yourself on deeper levels. Journal on: What did you discover about yourself? When you used your Goddess self-care toolkit to support you, how did you feel? What was your greatest achievement each season? Where did you find joy? Where did you find your calm? Celebrate your success with a little treat.

22 TUESDAY

23 WEDNESDAY

24 THURSDAY

Goddess Luna is calling you to soften more today. Take a few big breaths innnnnn and ouuuuut, let go and soften into your body even more. As you soften, you become more open to her whispers of insights coming through to you.

25 FRIDAY

Dreamy Fridays are a thing ... did you know?
   Luna sends the whispers of love, inspiration, wisdom and clarity to you while you dream this weekend. Listen out for them and try to remember what she said when you wake.

26 SATURDAY

27 SUNDAY

September

SELENE

Your Moon Goddess for September is Selene.

Selene is a Greek Goddess of the Moon. She is ethereal, stunningly beautiful and she really owns and loves her whole body. Selene wears a crescent moon crown of sparkling rose gold, colored bangles, and a dress that skims her body and enhances her hourglass figure beautifully. Her dress is long and touches the ground as Selene moves around the moon.

Selene has dark hair gathered on top of her head with some curls loosely falling out around her face. She has soft, brown skin and deep brown eyes.

She is sending out a stream of moonlight from her hand to light up the darkness.

Selene is the goddess of peace, intuition, gut wisdom, beauty and time. She embodies a calm, serene and tranquil state; she sees beauty in every living creature, in every moment; and she is a deeply respected healer. Selene has come through this month to support you to connect to your calm, see your beauty more and heal your wounds of judging your body that she can feel you are carrying.

Selene's mantra is 'I am learning that my body is beautiful and divine, just as it is.'

Her crystals are obsidian, tourmaline and malachite.

Her totem is the crow and the darkness – she embodies the magic of the darkness.

Her exercises are dancing, stretching and strength training.

Her scents are spicy scents such as pepper, cinnamon and chili – for spicing up your life.

28 MONDAY

Sometimes, a Full Moon approaches with a gentle energy and you start to notice what's stirring a day or two out, and sometimes, she comes in with her lights on high beam, all powerful and potent. You can feel the stirrings of what she is saying (or insisting, it seems) to clear, to cleanse, to heal, days out from her reaching her fullness.

This Pisces Blue Moon reaches her fullness on Thursday and she sure seems to be insisting on attention. Being a watery moon, it's a rather emotional time, so random acts of crying are to be expected and honored. Use your self-care toolkit and call in support from the Goddess Luna.

29 TUESDAY

30 WEDNESDAY

31 THURSDAY ○

Oh, feel into this new energy of the Full Blue Moon today. This gorgeous and powerful Blue Moon in Pisces sure has been stirring things up over the last couple of days.

   The water signs are all controllers of our emotions, so they really bring to the surface the emotions you have been holding onto, or that you need to clear and cleanse, so you can move forward from a place of letting go. Best question for this moon is: What am I leaving behind?

   It's an incredibly potent time to meditate, journal, or have a ritual bath or fire during this Full Moon, so you may ready yourself to stand in your radiance, your potency, as you move into fall 2023.

1 FRIDAY

Any twirling as you walk through your day will add extra credit points toward miracles ... take the twirl!!

2 SATURDAY

3 SUNDAY

4 MONDAY

5 TUESDAY

Selene is sending you sparkles of moonlight to fill up your whole body with beautiful healing and inspiring light. Breathe it in!

6 WEDNESDAY ◐

7 THURSDAY

8 FRIDAY

With just a few more weeks to use your Goddess self-care toolkit, squeeze in and soak up those last fragments of support. Play your songs, wear your color, smell your fragrance, move your body and use your crystal energy as much as you can, to turn up the volume of receiving support.

9 SATURDAY

10 SUNDAY

11 MONDAY

If you looked back on what you have achieved during summer, what would you notice?
Can you see what you have accomplished? Write it down so you can be reminded of what
you have done well. And then, celebrate your success and your courageous spirit by doing
something special for yourself. What will you do or buy, or how could you treat yourself?

12 TUESDAY

13 WEDNESDAY

14 THURSDAY

The dark night before the New Moon brings you the opportunity to take a last pause before the New Moon begins tomorrow. Feeling really tired is normal around this time in the moon cycle. Have you noticed that? Does your bedtime need adjusting tonight? It's a great time for an easy dinner, clearing off your bedside table, having extra water, essential oil and snuggles in bed with a person, pillow, animal or teddy. What do you need today?

15 FRIDAY ●

As you wake to the beginning of this beautiful New Moon cycle, this new expansive energy, you start to take those first tentative steps into your day ...

Remember, you've got this today.

Remember, the whole universe is conspiring to bring your dreams into reality.

Remember, all your angels and Goddess Selene are cheering you on, as you take those small baby steps forward.

Remember, you are grounded into the beautiful Virgo moon energy.

Remember, Mother Earth is with you, deepening your connection to the sacred earth wisdom and the nature spirits.

Remember, everyone believes in you!

16 SATURDAY

17 SUNDAY

18 MONDAY

19 TUESDAY

Your mission this week is to discover what your favorite flower is for fall and to draw it, paint it, or print it out and stick it into your diary. Sprinkle your flower all over the pages.

20 WEDNESDAY

21 THURSDAY

And as if by magic, the wheel of the seasons turns, shifting the energy into the new delights of fall for you. What do you love most about fall? How will you prioritize giving this to yourself over the next 12 weeks?

22 FRIDAY

Today is a big, potent and beautiful day of celebration. It's the Fall Equinox. The Fall Equinox is an ancient celebration, where the day and night are equal in length, and balance and harmony become infused throughout your world.

It's about recognising the 'harvest of your life' – all those things that you have created throughout your life. Look around at your body, your home, your workplace, your outside space, your whole life and see all the wonderful things that fill your world. Really feel the gratitude for what is in your life today.

It is a beautiful day to burn some incense around your home and your body, clearing your path forward for the fall season.

23 SATURDAY

24 SUNDAY

25 MONDAY

26 TUESDAY

Time to do your new Goddess self-care toolkit – jump over now and let's do this!

27 WEDNESDAY

28 THURSDAY

29 FRIDAY ○

Oh hello, gorgeous one. Yeah you, the spunky one who is here today in all your radiant glory.

It's a Full Moon today in the fiery sign of Aries; take a big breath and connect into her energy, her strength, her fullness. Place your hand on your heart and really feel a gentle softening there ... that's it.

This Full Moon is urging you to purge and clear away what is no longer in your highest good to carry. Journal on: What is holding you back? What is in your way? Where are you not doing *you* first?

Allow this moon to fire you up from deep within your heart and call in that sacred warrior strength of the Goddess Selene to inspire your baby steps forward in the direction of your dreams.

30 SATURDAY

1 SUNDAY

MY GODDESS SELF-CARE TOOLKIT FOR FALL

Fall is the time to turn inward, retreat and enjoy the change of the season, the weather temperature cooling and the change in seasonal foods.

Set your intentions for the next 12 weeks, which will be a time for you to honor your space, set your boundaries, and a great time for healing and meditation. This is also a perfect time to snuggle in, a time to journal and definitely a time for taking long baths with a fabulous book.

Have a look back at the toolkit you created for summer and note how it has supported you. Did you use your tools to their full potential or does something need a little adjustment? Send each of your tools a big heartfelt thank you for supporting you throughout the summer.

You outgrow things that support you because you are always changing and growing and shifting. You will find yourself choosing different tools to support you for this season.

With tingles of excitement deep in your belly, let's get started!

All the self-care tools you choose here will support you from today until the Winter Solstice in December. These self-care tools will help you to shine through your fall season with extra sprinkles of love and magic.

There are no right or wrong answers. Let go of your answers being any better, for they are all just your perfectly imperfect answers for today. Take five big breaths, really filling up your lungs, then let all your breath out. Imagine a slippery dip is going from your thinking mind into your heart space. Feel yourself sliding down and landing in your heart. Open your heart space a little wider (even if you are unsure if you're doing it right, trust that you are) – that's it!

GODDESS

Let's start with choosing a goddess. Flip through until you come to October, November and December. Really notice the picture of each goddess and read the description about her. Which goddess feels like she will help you the most this season?

The goddess I have chosen to support me throughout fall 2023 is

_____

She will support me with the medicine of her

_____

COLOR

Choose one color that is going to support you throughout fall. Land on your color and write it down here:

_____

When I see this color, I feel

_____

I can use this color to support me throughout fall with things such as clothing, accessories, jewelry, flowers, scatter cushions, candles, crystals, pens and

_____

SONGS

Choose three upbeat songs. Songs that you love, songs that get you up and moving, songs that make you feel that it's impossible to stay completely still, songs that make you feel like you want to boom-shakka-lakka and shimmy-shake around your house.

When you feel irritated, what could you do to get those deep irritations and emotions out of your body? You can dance them out! Yes, I know it sounds a little bit weird (okay, super weird) but it really does work.

If I am feeling a little triggered, angry, scared, irritated or just in a funk, I can play these three songs so I can get all loose and not caring, and allow the music and dance to move me through the emotion.

My three songs are:

1. _____

2. _____

3. _____

Your song mission is to download your three songs and create a special fall playlist on your phone so that, whenever you need them, they are ready for you.

EXERCISE

Don't moan when you read the word 'exercise'. It will be okay, I promise. Moving your body is important: you know that, I know that, everyone knows that. If there was a magical place that you could visit and it would transform your body with the push of a button, we'd all go there, right? Unfortunately, I am yet to discover this place so, for now, we all have to move our bodies to keep them strong and bendy, in the ways we have available to us at this moment.

Make this exercise as joyful, pleasurable, enlightening and as fun as it can be. There are so many ways to move your body. Choose one that feels exciting for you now.

The ways I will move my body during fall are:

_____

I will do these at _____ (location), _____ times per week.

FRAGRANCE

Your nose is a powerful tool. When you smell something you love, your whole body can feel so happy. It is like your nose holds this secret power to connect you to what brings you pleasure. You even have memories triggered by your sense of smell. In choosing to notice these scents you love, and by sprinkling them throughout your day, you will trigger a pleasure response that reminds you to feel all loved up and amazing. Kinda cool, hey!

For fall choose one smell that is going to support you throughout this season. It could be an essential oil, a perfume, a flower. Choose something you just love, that is easy to use and fills you with pleasure.

Land on your fragrance and write it down here:

_____

When your nostrils are tickled with this fragrance, how do you feel?

_____

I can use this fragrance as my signature fall scent to support me in lots of ways, such as burning essential oils and candles, using in skincare, eating or cooking with it, wearing the perfume, smelling fresh flowers, as well as

_____ and _____

CRYSTALS

Crystals are like magical particles that hold healing powers within. There are thousands of crystals available and they all have individual characteristics or ways to support you. Using the magic of one crystal helps to guide you with what you are working on, with healing, clearing energy or reminding you how you are growing and what you are wanting to step into.

The crystal that I am choosing to support me for fall is called

_____

It is _____ (color) and it will help me to _____

I can use this crystal to support me in lots of ways, such as carrying a piece in my pocket, or keeping a piece in the car or my bag. I could wear it in jewelry, use it as a screensaver on my phone, pop it under my pillow or mattress to support me while I sleep, or I could

_____ or _____

MANTRA

You know what you are working on and how you would like to feel. Have a look at the goddesses from October, November and December. Choose one of the mantras they have sent to you.

I am learning how to

_____

Your special mantra mission is to write your affirmation on post-it notes and sprinkle these words around your home, work office, phone and car. Write it down every week in this diary until the Winter Solstice to remind you to say it. Write it in lipstick on your mirror or in your journal, or perhaps you could

_____

For an extra gold star for being amazing, fill in three things you love most about fall.

1. _____

2. _____

3. _____

I will choose to do these things more because they bring me pleasure and fill my heart with joy. I deserve joy. (Yes, you really do!)

Well done. That is your very own Goddess self-care toolkit for fall all finished and completed. It will be here to support you through to the Winter Solstice in December.

Call in your goddess and play your three boppy songs now, swaying those hips as you dance and twirl around in celebration of completing your toolkit.

October

ANAHITA

Your Moon Goddess for October is Anahita.

Anahita is a Persian Moon Goddess of water, love, beauty, relationships, sexuality and fertility – she is the creator and giver of life, who pours healing waters throughout the world.

She is incredibly passionate, energetic and oozes confidence in who she is. Anahita wears a traditional dress with highlights of beads and golden thread, that hug against her volumptuous curves.

She wears a tiara of precious jewels with gold, rubies, diamonds and sapphires adorning her wrists and fingers. Anahita allows life to support her on all levels and trusts in the flow of abundance. She uses peacock feathers to bring in the medicine of being proudly herself and a little bit showy. She is young, ripe and has the energy of the maiden.

Anahita is the goddess who teases out of you the confident, fertile, feminine and beautiful woman inside – and she invites you to dance with her on the moon.

Anahita's mantra is 'I am learning to passionately choose my joy and pleasure first.'

Her crystals are diamonds, citrine and carnelian.

Her totem is bells to use in twinkling and ringing in your magic.

Her exercises are belly dancing, singing and moving your body to music.

Her scents are alluring fragrances such as jasmine, mandarin, ylang ylang, sandalwood and cardamon.

2 MONDAY

Your mantra from Anahita is: 'I am learning to passionately choose my joy and pleasure first.'
Where can you pop it up or write it each day in your diary, so you remember?

3 TUESDAY

4 WEDNESDAY

5 THURSDAY

Because Anahita loves bells to ring in your magic, could you make tingling bells your ringtone for October, to jingle in your joy, pleasure and magic?

6 FRIDAY ◑

7 SATURDAY

8 SUNDAY

Weave in the medicine of diamonds and peacock feathers with Anahita. Call them into your space, your body and your day. The diamonds are to remind you of your precious and rare gifts sparkling out into the world, and the peacock feathers are for showing these gifts to others. You are sacred.

9 MONDAY

10 TUESDAY

11 WEDNESDAY

As the energy continues to build in this potent dark moon phase and solar eclipse, you may be feeling tired, angry or irritated; needing to pull away and retreat; having lucid or lots of dreams; feeling moody and having disrupted sleep; or craving alone time this weekend. Choose something in your Goddess self-care toolkit to support you. What do you need today?

12 THURSDAY

13 FRIDAY

You have a solar eclipse tomorrow that is illuminating and shining its bright light onto any areas of your life that need some extra attention. It's a time of replenishing, so feeling drained, really tired and needing to jump into bed early is completely normal. Notice your dreams; there may be some messages there for you.

Enjoy this sacred time, accepting what is being lit up, pausing for reflection (that can be tricky!) and taking the time to go within.

14 SATURDAY

Today brings you a New Moon in the airy sign of Libra. The planet Venus is ruled by Libra, so relationships and love are the themes of this New Moon time. It's a great time to explore your current relationships, noticing what works, what needs adjusting and what you would like to move on from.

You have so many relationships in your life, so go wider than just your romantic relationship. Remembering the relationship you have with yourself, you know, that gorgeous one who stares back at you each day in the mirror! What needs to change so you nurture and love her (him) as a priority?

15 SUNDAY

16 MONDAY

17 TUESDAY

Remember to just look up in the sky, knowing that Grandmother Moon and Goddess Anahita are there, sending you more love than you could possibly hold. This flow never stops. Breathe it into your body.

18 WEDNESDAY

19 THURSDAY

20 FRIDAY

21 SATURDAY

22 SUNDAY

Your desires matter; filling up your container
with so much peace, joy, gratitude, pleasure,
grace, flow, color, balance allows you to flow
out even more to those around you. What do
you need today? Dance it in.

23 MONDAY

24 TUESDAY

25 WEDNESDAY

In the space between eclipses, the energy can feel a little intense and uncomfortable. So, if you are feeling triggered, overwhelmed, confused or exhausted, try catching up with friends, dancing out the irritation, gardening or getting all creative and arty.

26 THURSDAY

27 FRIDAY

28 SATURDAY ○

Happy Full Moon and Partial Lunar Eclipse Day.

Eclipses open healing portals, which can be uncomfortable to move through but the rewards on the other side are always worth the struggle.

This month, the Full Moon falls in the earthy sign of Taurus. The sign of practicality, stability, reliability, staying true to your beliefs, and has a beautiful sensual energy.

Expand into this divine Full Moon lunar eclipse energy; throw your arms out with gratitude, knowing how supported and grounded you are right now with those big, strong tree roots, deep and wide into the earth, so you remain strong. Stay excited for the shift into your more, my more, the more for your country, your world – the more for us all. You are ready!

29 SUNDAY

November

FREYA

Your Moon Goddess for November is Freya.

Freya is the Viking or Norse Goddess of love, beauty and sexuality. She is charming, confident and deeply owns her intuition, her femininity and who she is. She's a bad-ass. Freya isn't a Moon Goddess in the traditional sense, because Gods were connected to the moon in Norse tradition, but she is such a beautiful energy to work with that she had to be included in this diary.

Freya is incredibly beautiful, empowered and confident. She is petite, yet strong, sexy and powerful in presence and of body; she looks fit with some minor muscle definition. Her dress is long, and she wears an amber amulet around her neck. From her hair dangles feathers, beads and bones in decoration.

She uses the phases of the moon to connect deeper to the arts of magic, astrology and plant medicine.

Freya has come through this month to support you to stand proudly as you are and to begin the journey of owning your story of creation, all those parts of who you are that make up you. Each tiny journey, each tiny particle that makes you whole – to be proud of that.

Freya's mantra is 'I am learning who I am. Right in this moment, I own my story.'

Her crystals are amethyst, rubies, amber and pink tourmaline.

Her totems are the bear, wolf, bones and cauldrons. She embodies the magic and medicine of nature.

Her exercises are walking through nature, swimming in bodies of water and climbing mountains.

Her scents are blends of all different essential oils made up to form sensual combination scents.

30 MONDAY

31 TUESDAY

The ancient celebrations of Halloween, Samhain and Day of the Dead all fall over the next few days, and the energy holds through your weekend. For however *you* choose to celebrate all or some of the sacred ceremonies ...

Know that the veil between realms is so thinly held right now, your ancestors and your spirit guide team *are* communicating with you and sending you signs of their presence in your life.

Know that magical things *are* being sprinkled throughout your life, stay on the lookout for them.

Know that blessings of love and light are flowing into your life, feel them coming through.

Know that, sometimes, the simplest ritual of lighting a candle and sending thanks and gratitude to all those who walk with you and cheer you on in this lifetime is enough. Keep it simple and loving.

1 WEDNESDAY

2 THURSDAY

Happy Day of the Dead, or *Dia de los Muertos*. Send your love and heartfelt gratitude out to all your ancestors for guiding you, supporting you and walking with you this year as you moved with the power of their presence and their song, celebrating all of who you are and honoring just how far you've come. Light a candle and say thank you to each of them.

3 FRIDAY

To feel your connection to the earth in a stronger, more supportive way this coming weekend, what do you need? Walks in nature, surfing, yoga on the grass, a picnic, gardening with your hands in the earth. What will support you to reconnect?

4 SATURDAY

5 SUNDAY

6 MONDAY

Grounding is such a simple practice and perhaps, because of this, it can be overlooked. Be like the big, strong, ancient tree. Send out your tree roots from the soles of your feet, deep and wide into the earth, through all the layers of the deep earth, too. Stable, connected and strong today, that's you.

7 TUESDAY

8 WEDNESDAY

9 THURSDAY

Your pleasure matters ... How can you claim that statement with more sparkle and pizazz today? How can you infuse more of what lights you up from deep within into your day?

Where can you give yourself permission to sprinkle more things in your life that make you smile?

It's doing the little things that sometimes matter the very most. Intentionally choosing to do what you love, your way, because you deserve to be filled with joy, pleasure and love bubbles.

10 FRIDAY

11 SATURDAY

12 SUNDAY

The dark night before the New Moon brings you the opportunity to take a last pause before the New Moon begins tomorrow. Feeling tired is normal around this time in the moon cycle. Do you have a special desire today? What is it? How can you give yourself that to feel an extra dose of love?

13 MONDAY ●

As the New Moon unfolds herself from the darkness of the shadows and gradually, gently, starts to shine and sparkle ... so too will you.

This gorgeous New Moon falls in the watery sign of Scorpio; it's a deep moon of transformation and rebirth, calling you to move into the depths of your shadow side. What has been coming up for you over the last week or so? What have you noticed? What needs to be cleared so you may let go, especially on an emotional level?

To transform into your new self, an old, outdated version must 'die'. Journal, sit in nature, meditate or find your stillness, and ask the question: 'What am I choosing to let go of?'

Allow the old to be held and loved for its wisdom and knowledge, then let it release and die.

14 TUESDAY

15 WEDNESDAY

Freya is supporting you to explore your life in deep ways and that can be tricky. You can do this. Use the power of Freya and this New Moon, and stand in its flow, allowing it to support you in your transformation, insights and rebirth. Like the phoenix who rises from the ashes – so too shall you.

16 THURSDAY

17 FRIDAY

18 SATURDAY

Where is your magic to be found, you
wonder? Freya will help you ... go find a
mirror and look deeply into your eyes.
There it is, there is your magic.

19 SUNDAY

20 MONDAY ◑

This time of year can have you feeling like you are being pulled in a thousand different directions, so it's really important to use your Goddess self-care toolkit to keep you out of the drama. This is so you can make decisions from your empowered self, rather than doing everything to please everyone else. What do you need today to support you? Now do that!

21 TUESDAY

22 WEDNESDAY

23 THURSDAY

What can you be grateful for today?

Nah not all the 'normal' things like your car, house, kids and job ... let's do a cool gratitude list of things about the most wonderful person in your life, you. Yep let's make it about her. And we are going to write out three – one physical, one abundance and one of your superpowers!

1. With a whole body filled with gratitude and bubbles of love I am thankful for my _____ because they help me to _____
2. With a whole body filled with gratitude and bubbles of love I am thankful for _____ because they allow me to_____
3. With a whole body filled with gratitude and bubbles of love I am thankful for my superpowers of _____ because they help me to be amazing at _____

Hands on your heart and take a big breath in of all your amazingness.

24 FRIDAY

Owning all your parts is what makes you whole. Let go of any annoying doubts that bubble up, for you are equally as ethereal and as gorgeous as Freya is. You just needed to be reminded.

25 SATURDAY

26 SUNDAY

27 MONDAY ○

Happy Full Moon day, oh radiant one. This Full Moon falls in the airy sign of Gemini, the sign of the mind. It's intellectual and dreamy; it's your thoughts, intuition and the balance of both your connection to this world and to the spirit realms.

It's a perfect time to use the potency of this moon to wash, clear and cleanse anything stuck or stagnant in your body. Using Freya's powers of magic, whoosh and whiz out the old limiting beliefs, stories, traumas, drama, the overthinking it all, and the getting carried away with negative thought patterns.

Stand under this moon (or through the window) and just bathe in the vitality, the power and magic of this time. Ask her to settle your mind. Ground in with those big, strong tree roots and just breathe it all in, trusting that, in the space you have created, you are in your perfect place and receiving on every level. Oh yeah ... that feels so special.

28 TUESDAY

29 WEDNESDAY

30 THURSDAY

Your joy matters and when you connect to this part of you ... this is when the magic happens.
Freya reminds you to play more today from the sensual, sexy side of you.

It's flirting with life.
It's flirting with yourself.
It's flirting with your reflection.
It's flirting with the wind.

1 FRIDAY

2 SATURDAY

3 SUNDAY

HINA HINE

Your Moon Goddess for December is Hina Hine.

Hina Hine is a Polynesian Goddess of the Moon. Hina is this incredibly beautiful goddess, who was tasked with saving the life of the moon. Hina sits on the moon, bathing in its healing waters as she lovingly gazes and watches over the earth from her high vantage point in the sky.

Hina swims in the sacred moon waters, bathing her body in the moon's healing. One of her favorite things to do is to swim naked on the moon with a tiara of hibiscus flowers in her hair.

Hina has this beautiful connection to herself as she sits in the solitude of deep reflection. She is deeply connected to the inner part of who she is, her femininity and her mystical gifts. She shines a light for you this month, supporting you to rediscover your hidden gifts, your connection to yourself and your mystical capabilities.

Hina's mantra is 'I am learning to surrender deeper and find my inner calm.'

Her crystals are larimar, aquamarine, moonstone and chrysocolla.

Her totems are shells, driftwood, herbs, flowers and plant medicine.

Her exercise is swimming in the ocean, allowing the waves to wash over and caress her body.

Her scents are all different essential oils — herbaceous, floral and woods — made up to form a powerful blend for meditative and intuitive insights.

4 MONDAY

If you looked back on what you have achieved during fall what would you notice? Can you see
what you have accomplished? Write it down, so you can be reminded what you have done
well. Then celebrate your success and your courageous spirit by doing something special for
yourself. What will you do or buy, or how could you treat yourself?

5 TUESDAY

6 WEDNESDAY

Hina Hine sends you the gentle flow of the ocean today. She asks you to set a timer for two
whole minutes and breathe, just let go and trust today that you are supported.

7 THURSDAY

8 FRIDAY

9 SATURDAY

10 SUNDAY

What do you love about Christmas time?
What is your Christmas story of magic, joy
and pleasure? Endless slices of Christmas
ham, watching your children leave out
special treats for Santa, time with family,
carols, Christmas lights twinkling from
houses, school holidays, Love Actually,
snuggling under the covers, less traffic on
weekdays, winter walks through nature, Santa
hats, mistletoe, trifle, sleep-ins, snow angels,
opening presents ...

Add to this list to remind you of all the joy
that can be found at this time of year!!

11 MONDAY

12 TUESDAY

Today brings a beautiful shift, as the moon turns that little bit more and shimmers onto the earth. It's New Moon time in the fiery sign of Sagittarius. This New Moon brings you the firing up, the motivation and the passion to define what you want your last few weeks of this year to feel like.

What do want? What do you really want more of in your life? Use the fire element to burn off anything that feels in the way of you getting to decide what you want.

Stretch out, tease out your desires so you begin the journey of trusting yourself more each day to choose your pleasure, your freedom, your joy.

The 12th day of the 12th month, 12:12, opens up a beautiful healing gateway each year. This year is extra potent because it falls on the dark night of the moon. Surrender into this day, imagining beautiful healing rays are being sent down on and through your body. Swim, bathe or dance in the healing with the Goddess Hina.

13 WEDNESDAY

14 THURSDAY

15 FRIDAY

16 SATURDAY

17 SUNDAY

As fall draws to a close, look back on the last 12 weeks and notice the ways you have connected to yourself on deeper levels. Journal on: What did you discover about yourself? When you used your Goddess self-care toolkit to support you, how did you feel? What was your greatest achievement this season? Where did you find joy? Where did you find your calm?

18 MONDAY

Hina Hine guides your mission this week. She sends you to discover what your favorite smell of winter 2023 is: cinnamon, pine trees, a burning fire, cookies baking, ginger, the forest, hot chocolate, which one is tickling your nostrils with extra love this year? I wonder what you will find!

19 TUESDAY ◑

20 WEDNESDAY

The wheel of the seasons turn once more, shifting the energy into winter for you. Winter is the season of rest and replenishing, so you may be reborn in the spring stronger and ready to bloom forth. Winter can often be the hardest season to navigate through, because often, we struggle to take the time to just be, to look inside and contract in.

What is your relationship with rest, surrendering to what is and not pushing forward? The difference for you will be that, this winter, you have your Goddess self-care toolkit and your guide Goddess Hina ready to support you through this season.

Journal on what you love most about winter.

21 THURSDAY

22 FRIDAY

Today is the Winter Solstice, a day that begins the new light of the sun's energy. It's the cycle that starts with the shortest day, and the longest and darkest night. It's like a rebirthing of the sun's energy. Create the space to look at what you want and what you want to bring to life during the rest of your year. Just like in nature, you can start to nurture your dreams, birthing them into reality in spring.

It's a beautiful time to use the fire element in ritual – light a candle or dance around a fire with the desire to burn away the next layer of anything you are choosing not to carry into the rest of 2023. It's a sacred time to shine your light on your own life, stepping into your empowered place of balance, alignment to the seasons, grounded strength and inner wisdom. You are learning to deeply and lovingly express your potency.

23 SATURDAY

Time to do your new Goddess self-care toolkit, using the power and magic of the ocean. Jump over to your new Moon Goddess Dairy 2024, and let's do this together.

24 SUNDAY

25 MONDAY

The sleigh bells are ringing, their jingle is in the air. Are you listening? Deck the Halls with your dancing and magic ... if it's a Silent Night, find your silence within ... if you are in a Winter Wonderland, may you dream unafraid ... and I do hope you have yourself a Merry Little Christmas, knowing what a Joy to the World you really are.

26 TUESDAY

27 WEDNESDAY ○

Happy Full Moon, darling one. This month, she falls in the watery sign of Cancer. Cancer's ruling planet is the moon, which makes the energy a little more obvious – we all feel it more. As the last Full Moon of 2023, there is a strong element to cleanse and purge anything you are choosing to let go of before the New Year begins.

What can you move through your body, flush through your body, clear from your home or cleanse from your space over the next few days?

This moon has such a potent connection to the divine feminine and divine mother. You are being asked to nurture yourself by loving your depths, your scars, your journey this year, your journey to now. Connect to the water: drink more, watch the rain, dance in the rain, wander by the water, and swim through it to hold and nourish all of you.

28 THURSDAY

29 FRIDAY

30 SATURDAY

31 SUNDAY

Darling one, it is radiant and extra sparkly moonbeams of love that I send to you for sharing your journey through 2023 with me. It is an honor to hold this sacred space for you as you learn to weave in your magic through your life.

Here's to a spectacular, magical and abundant 2024 together ... let's do this!

Nicci xx

RITUAL TO CLOSE OFF THE YEAR 2023

As you close off the year and begin to walk a new path into the new journey of 2024, create a little space to do this ritual...

Today, I send gratitude to the path I walked this year, the experiences I had, the people I shared this adventure with. I am so thankful for the learnings I received and the wisdom I called upon from my moon goddesses and from deep inside myself to support me more.

I send thanks to all my angels, my spirits guides, Mother Earth, the seasons, the planets and the moon for holding me as I moved through this year.

I am here today, on the last day of this year, because I made it through all those tough times, the challenges, the deep ravines of sadness and trauma, the endless mountains of hardship and uncertainty. I kept swimming through the oceans of pain and fear. I kept moving and walking and pivoting through it all. I chose to keep going, gosh, I'm so proud of me.

Now, put your hands on your hips, broaden your chest, raise your chin and take a big, deep breath. Now keep reading!

I realize now that I am rather amazing! I see that, more clearly than I have before.

I am ready to see my magnificence so much more in 2024.

I am ready to use my gifts and talents to support myself and to sprinkle my magic through the world.

My vision will be clear and profound as I follow my dreams, my groove, my light, my way.

I am allowing my life to stay open to the unexpected sprinkles of magic, laughter, joy and wonder throughout 2024. I am ready for my 'more'.

Now, happy dance yourself with all the songs you chose to support you this year from your Goddess self-care toolkits, swinging into your BEST year yet, you spunky and oh-so gorgeous thang!

Grab your 2024 diary now, so you can feel extra supported and held while you learn how to come back to your sacred gifts and talents, your mission, your purpose ... your self.

I'll be there to support you.

With big smooches,

Nicci x

NB: All moon times and planetary movements used through this diary are set to Greenwich Mean Time (GMT). To convert times to exactly where you are located in the world, I suggest using www.timeanddate.com. Moon and planetary interpretations consider all aspects of where the moon, the sun, the astrological signs and the planets fall on each day and are not taken out of context.

A Rockpool book
PO Box 252
Summer Hill
NSW 2130, Australia

rockpoolpublishing.com
Follow us! �f 📷 rockpoolpublishing
Tag your images with #rockpoolpublishing

ISBN: 9781922579171

Published in 2022 by Rockpool Publishing
Design by Sara Lindberg, Rockpool Publishing
Edited by Brooke Halliwell

Printed and bound in China
10 9 8 7 6 5 4 3 2 1

This diary is dedicated to you.

Yep, that's right, a whole book made for you.

For being just as you are, right in that
very breath, right in that very smile.

You are completely that special
and I am honoured to be sharing
this adventure of life with you.

It's all for you, baby!

With rivers of love and mountains of magic.

Nicci xx